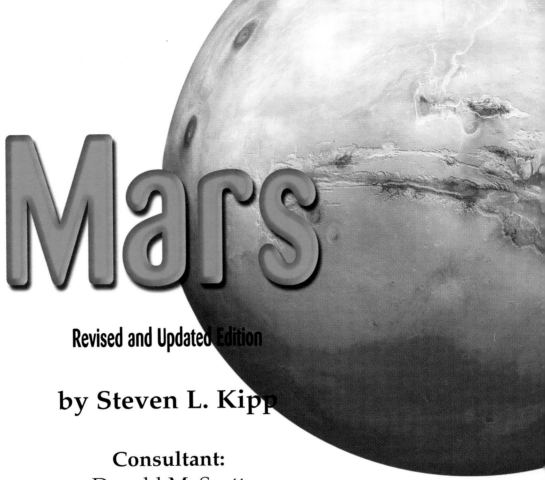

Mars

Revised and Updated Edition

by Steven L. Kipp

Consultant:
Donald M. Scott
Aerospace Education Specialist
Oklahoma State University and
NASA Ames Research Center

Bridgestone Books
an imprint of Capstone Press
Mankato, Minnesota

Bridgestone Books are published by Capstone Press
151 Good Counsel Drive, P.O. Box 669, Mankato, Minnesota 56002
http://www.capstone-press.com

Library of Congress Cataloging-in-Publication Data
The Library of Congress has cataloged the first edition as follows:
Kipp, Steven L.
    Mars/by Steven L. Kipp.
    p. cm.—(The galaxy)
    Includes bibliographical references and index.
    Summary: Discusses the surface features, atmosphere, exploration, and other aspects
of the planet Mars.
    ISBN 0-7368-0520-6
    1. Mars (Planet)—Juvenile literature. [1. Mars (Planet)] I. Title. II. Series.
QB641.K35 1998
523.43—dc21
                                                                                97-6922
                                                                                CIP

Editorial Credits
Tom Adamson, editor; Timothy Halldin, cover designer and illustrator; Kimberly Danger
    and Jodi Theisen, photo researchers

Photo Credits
NASA, cover, 8, 10, 12, 13, 14, 16, 18
NASA/JPL/Malin Space Science Systems, 20
U.S. Geological Survey, Flagstaff, AZ, 1, 6

1 2 3 4 5 6 05 04 03 02 01 00

Table of Contents

Relative size of the Sun and the planets

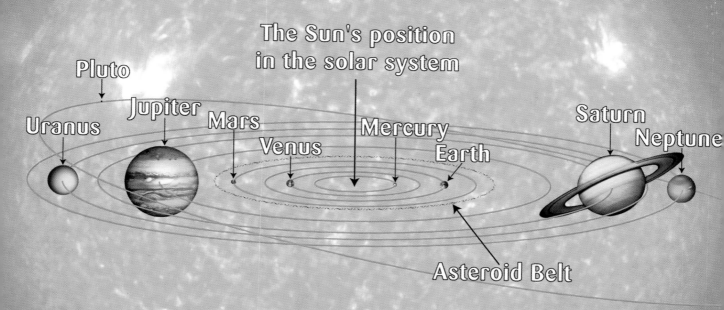

The Sun's position in the solar system

Pluto

Uranus

Jupiter

Mars

Venus

Mercury

Earth

Saturn

Neptune

Asteroid Belt

The Sun

Mars is a planet in the solar system. The Sun is the center of the solar system. Planets, asteroids, and comets travel around the Sun.

Mars is the fourth planet from the Sun. It is about 142 million miles (228 million kilometers) away from the Sun. Mars is one of the four rocky inner planets. Mercury, Venus, and Earth are the other inner planets.

Four outer planets are much larger than the inner planets. Jupiter, Saturn, Uranus, and Neptune are made of gases. Pluto is the farthest planet from the Sun. This small planet is made of rock and ice.

Scientists think that life may have existed on Mars long ago. They continue to study the planet to learn about its history.

◄ **This illustration compares the sizes of the planets and the Sun. Mars is the third smallest planet. The blue lines show the orbits of the planets. Thousands of asteroids move around the Sun. The asteroid belt is between the orbits of Mars and Jupiter.**

FAST FACTS

	Mars	Earth
Diameter:	4,222 miles (6,794 kilometers)	7,927 miles (12,756 kilometers)
Average distance from the Sun:	142 million miles (228 million kilometers)	93 million miles (150 million kilometers)
Revolution period:	687 days	365 days, 6 hours
Rotation period:	24 hours, 37 minutes	23 hours, 56 minutes
Moons:	2	1

◀ Mars has many large surface features. This picture shows the Valles Marineris canyon system. The spots on the left are huge volcanoes. These volcanoes are no longer active.

The Planet Mars

People can see Mars in the night sky during certain times of the year. From Earth, the planet looks like a bright red star. Through a telescope, Mars seems to look like Earth. Mars has polar caps and clouds. The planet has light and dark areas that change with the seasons.

Mars is smaller than Earth. Mars is 4,222 miles (6,794 kilometers) wide. Seven planets the size of Mars could fit into the planet Earth.

Until recently, astronomers knew little about Mars. Some people thought intelligent beings lived on Mars. They called these imagined life forms Martians. People wrote stories and made movies about Martians.

Today's scientists are working to learn more about Mars. They use powerful telescopes to look at the planet. They also have sent space probes to explore Mars. Scientists continue to search for clues that life once existed on Mars.

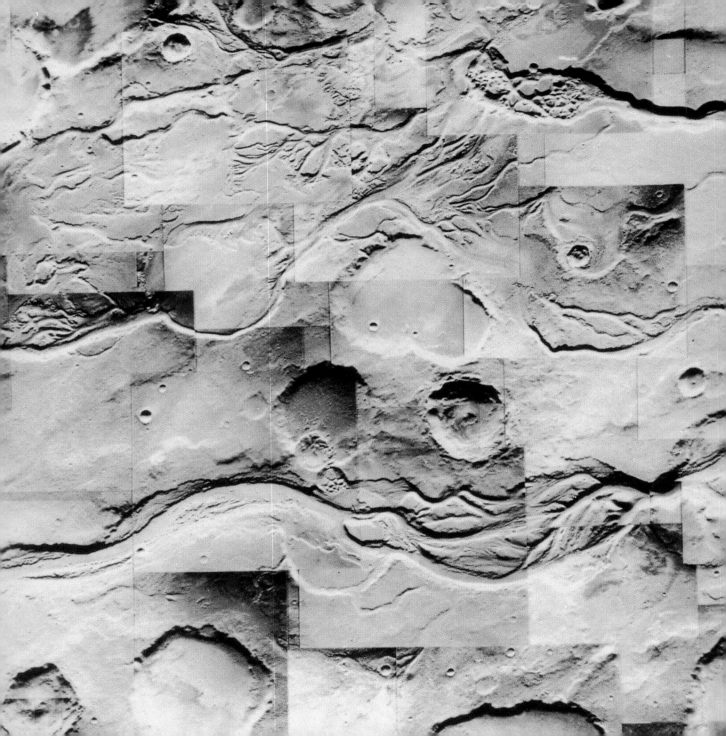

Canals

In the 1800s, an astronomer named Giovanni Schiaparelli studied Mars. Schiaparelli looked at Mars through a telescope.

Schiaparelli thought he saw lines on Mars. He called these lines canali. This Italian word can mean either river channels or canals made by people. River channels are natural riverbeds. Canals are channels for water that people dig through land.

Schiaparelli meant river channels. But people misunderstood. They thought he meant canals made by people. They thought Martians must have built the canals.

American astronomer Percival Lowell also studied Mars in the 1800s. He told people that he saw canals too. Lowell believed that Martians had dug the canals. He thought the canals carried water to Martian farmland.

Long ago, water may have flowed in these dry river channels on Mars.

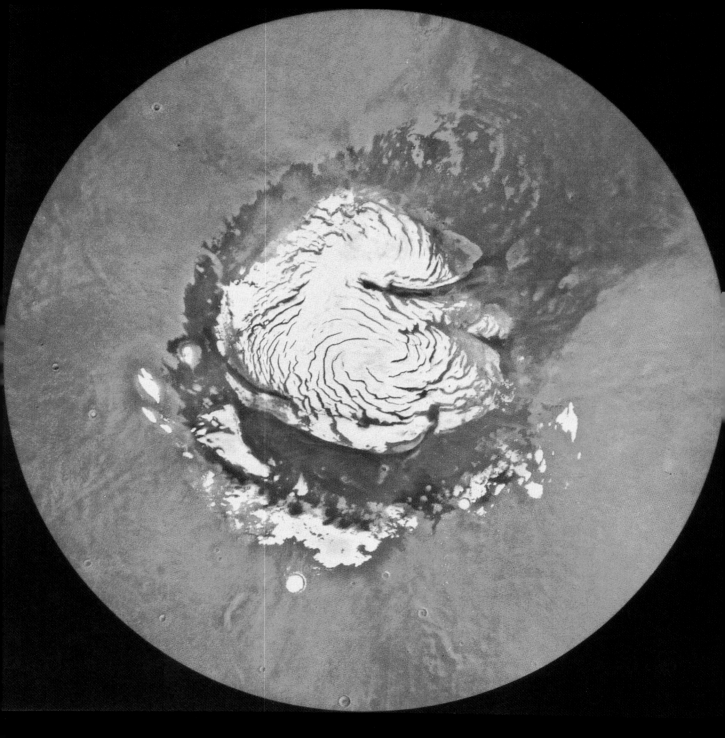

Mars's atmosphere is a thin layer of carbon dioxide gas. Mars's weak gravity keeps the atmosphere thin. Gravity is a force that pulls objects together. Mars's gravity is too weak to support a thick atmosphere. Most gases on Mars escape into outer space.

A planet's atmosphere holds in heat from the Sun. Mars becomes cold because its atmosphere is thin. Heat escapes into outer space. Mars's surface temperature can range from minus 200 degrees to 80 degrees above zero Fahrenheit (minus 130 degrees to 27 degrees above zero Celsius).

Mars becomes so cold that the carbon dioxide gas in the atmosphere freezes. The carbon dioxide turns into ice on the planet's surface. Frozen carbon dioxide is called dry ice. Most of this dry ice lies at Mars's north and south poles. During summer, some of the ice warms and turns into a gas. In winter, the gas freezes into ice again.

Frozen carbon dioxide, or dry ice, covers Mars's north and south poles.

Like all planets, Mars orbits the Sun. Each trip around the Sun is one revolution. Mars orbits the Sun once every 687 days.

Mars also rotates, or spins, as it orbits. Mars rotates once every 24 hours and 37 minutes. Earth rotates once every 23 hours and 56 minutes. One rotation is a day. The length of a day on Earth and a day on Mars is almost the same.

Scientists measure rotation time by finding a large feature on the surface of a planet. They measure the time and place they first see the feature. The feature rotates with the planet. Scientists measure the time the feature takes to complete a rotation. Mars rotates from west to east. Earth rotates in the same direction.

Features on a planet seem to move across the surface. They move because the planet rotates.

Two moons orbit Mars. An astronomer discovered Phobos and Deimos in 1877. In Greek and Roman myths, Phobos and Deimos were the sons of the god Mars.

Some astronomers think Phobos and Deimos are asteroids. These large space rocks orbit the Sun. Mars's gravity probably captured Phobos and Deimos.

Phobos is Mars's largest moon. Phobos is 17 miles (27 kilometers) across at its widest point. This moon orbits 3,700 miles (6,000 kilometers) above Mars's surface.

Deimos is only 9 miles (15 kilometers) across at its widest point. This moon orbits more than 12,400 miles (20,000 kilometers) above Mars's surface.

Phobos and Deimos probably are made up of rock with a layer of dust. Both moons have many craters. Asteroids crashed into the moons to form the craters.

Both Phobos and Deimos are shaped like potatoes. This picture of Phobos shows many craters on its surface.

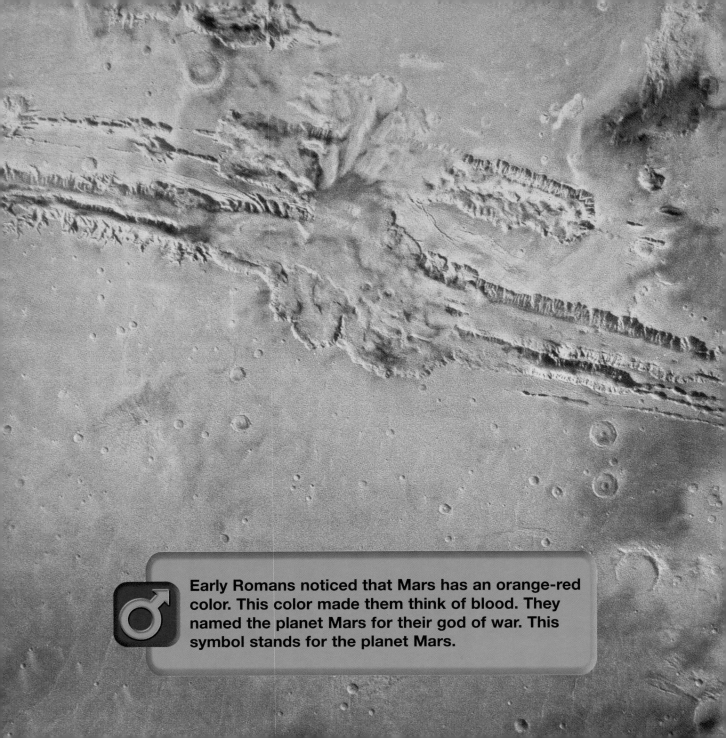

Early Romans noticed that Mars has an orange-red color. This color made them think of blood. They named the planet Mars for their god of war. This symbol stands for the planet Mars.

The northern part of Mars has many volcanoes. Flat plains lie between the volcanoes. Lava from volcanoes formed the plains. Craters, sand, and small rocks cover other parts of Mars.

The sand and small rocks are made of a mixture of iron and oxygen. Iron is a metal. Oxygen is a gas. The two items combine to make iron oxide, or rust. Iron oxide makes the sand and rocks on Mars orange-red. Strong winds on Mars blow the sand around. These strong winds sometimes cause large dust storms.

The Tharsis Bulge is near the middle of Mars. This area has four huge volcanoes that rise above the land. The giant Valles Marineris is near the Tharsis Bulge. Valles Marineris is a huge system of canyons. This system is more than 2,500 miles (4,000 kilometers) long.

Valles Marineris is as long as the distance between Los Angeles and New York City.

Space Probes

In 1972, scientists sent the *Mariner 9* space probe into orbit around Mars. With this space probe, scientists found the solar system's tallest and largest known volcano. Olympus Mons covers an area the size of Montana.

The *Viking 1* and *Viking 2* space probes landed on Mars in 1976. They took pictures of Mars's surface. These landers studied Mars's atmosphere, weather, and soil. Robotic arms scooped up Martian soil. Tests found no living things in the soil.

In 1997, *Pathfinder* landed on Mars. This space probe carried a rover called *Sojourner*. Scientists controlled this small vehicle from Earth. They sent signals through space to tell *Sojourner* where to go.

Sojourner explored the surface of Mars for more than two months. The rover studied the soil and several rocks. Scientists gave these rocks names such as Yogi, Barnacle Bill, and Scooby Doo. *Pathfinder* sent thousands of images of Mars back to Earth.

Scientific instruments on *Sojourner* tested several rocks. The tests showed that many rocks on Mars are similar to volcanic rocks on Earth.

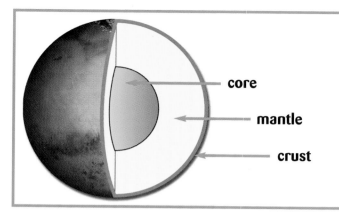

core

mantle

crust

Scientists believe Mars has three layers. The core is the innermost layer. The mantle surrounds the core. The mantle probably is made of liquid rock. A thin crust forms the planet's outer layer. Information from *Mars Global Surveyor* helps scientists learn what makes up the interior of Mars.

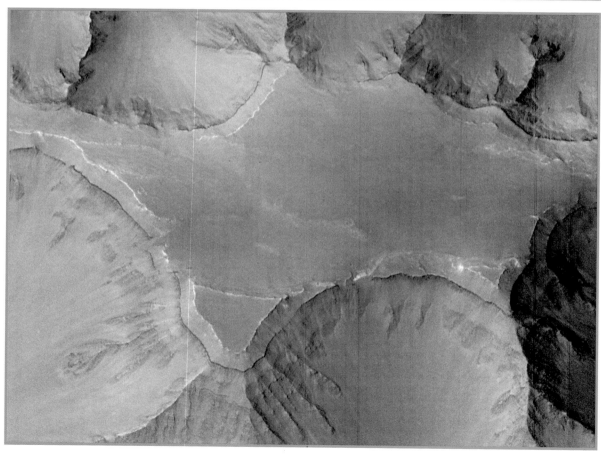

Recent and Future Missions

In 1997, *Mars Global Surveyor* began orbiting Mars. The *Surveyor*'s mission is to map the surface of Mars. The probe is providing the clearest pictures scientists have seen of Mars's surface. Studying Mars helps scientists learn more about Earth.

Scientists are planning new missions to Mars. They will send more landers and rovers to explore the planet. In the next mission, the *Marie Curie* rover is expected to explore Mars. This rover is similar to *Sojourner*.

In another mission, scientists plan to bring a sample of Martian soil to Earth. They will study this soil in laboratories to look for signs of life.

These missions will help scientists plan for a human mission to Mars. They want astronauts to explore Mars safely. Scientists hope to send astronauts to Mars by 2020.

Mars Global Surveyor took this picture of a part of the Valles Marineris.

Hands On: Make Martian Sand

The sand on Mars is orange-red. Iron oxide gives the sand its color. Iron oxide also is called rust. You can make your own Martian sand.

What You Need

Three large pieces of steel wool
Scissors
Pie plate
Sand
Water

What You Do

1. Cut the steel wool into small pieces.
2. Fill your pie plate half full with sand.
3. Mix the small pieces of steel wool with the sand.
4. Mix one cup of water with the sand and steel wool.

In a few days, your sand will look orange-red. The iron in the steel wool mixed with the oxygen in the water to make iron oxide. The iron oxide mixed with the sand as it does on Mars. You now have sand that is similar to the sand on Mars.

Words to Know

asteroid (ASS-tuh-roid)—a large space rock that orbits the Sun

astronomer (uh-STRON-uh-mer)—a person who studies the planets, stars, and space

atmosphere (AT-muhss-feehr)—the mixture of gases that surrounds some planets

orbit (OR-bit)—the path of an object as it travels around another object in space

revolution (rev-uh-LOO-shuhn)—the movement of one object around another object in space

rotation (roh-TAY-shuhn)—one complete spin of an object in space

space probe (SPAYSS PROHB)—a spacecraft that travels to other planets and outer space

telescope (TEL-uh-skope)—an instrument that makes faraway objects seem larger and closer

Read More

Brimner, Larry Dane. *Mars.* A True Book. New York: Children's Press, 1998.

Kerrod, Robin. *Astronomy.* Young Scientist Concepts and Projects. Milwaukee: Gareth Stevens, 1998.

Wunsch, Susi Trautmann. *The Adventures of Sojourner: The Mission to Mars that Thrilled the World.* New York: Mikaya Press, 1998.

Useful Addresses

Canadian Space Agency
6767 Route de l'Aéroport
Saint-Hubert, QC J3Y 8Y9
Canada

NASA Headquarters
Washington, DC 20546-0001

The Planetary Society
65 Catalina Avenue
Pasadena, CA 91106-2301

Internet Sites

The Center for Mars Exploration
http://cmex-www.arc.nasa.gov
Mars Exploration Program
http://mars.jpl.nasa.gov
The Nine Planets
http://www.tcsn.net/afiner

Index